WHAT, IF ANYTHING, IS OUT THERE?

WE MAY NOT BE ALONE

WHAT, IF ANYTHING, IS OUT THERE?

GENE P. ABEL
COL, USA RET.

Indigo River Publishing

Indigo River Publishing
3 West Garden Street, Ste. 718
Pensacola, FL 32502
www.indigoriverpublishing.com

What, If Anything, Is Out There? | Gene P. Abel, author
ISBN: 978-1-950906-89-5| LCCN: 2020922940

Edited by Earl Tillinghast
Cover and interior design by Robin Vuchnich

Special discounts are available on quantity purchases by corporations, associations, and others.

For details, contact the publisher at the address above. Orders by US trade bookstores and wholesalers: please contact the publisher at the address above.

With Indigo River Publishing, you can always expect great books, strong voices, and meaningful messages. Most importantly, you'll always find . . . words worth reading.

My sincere thanks to my beautiful wife, Susan Anne
for her help with my book.

Contents

INTRODUCTION

Man, for a long time, has sought to learn about his environment, other species, and most recently about other worlds and planets in the universe. This began many years ago when astronomers like Galileo first built telescopes to look into the heavens and see what was taking place.

We look at bees to see how they organize, and in so doing we have learned that they appear to communicate with each other and have developed a highly efficient society to propagate their species and live their lives. We watch migrant birds and see how they seem to know the changes in the seasons and follow a leader from one part of the earth to the other. We record the sounds of whales, who have a very distinct society and definitely appear to communicate with each other.

We have been interested in the deepest parts of the ocean and, with the technology that we have developed, have begun exploring such remote places as the Mariana Trench, which goes down almost seven miles. Due to these efforts, we have discovered life in our oceans like no other that we have ever seen before and even a few species that are not carbon-based. They exist in environments that would be toxic to other living creatures, around hydrothermal vents on the floor of the deepest parts of our oceans. The temperature at these vents ranges up to 700 degrees Fahrenheit, and the vents spew highly toxic sulfur compounds into the ocean. Despite conditions that would be deadly to almost all life on Earth, scientists have found huge, red-tipped tubeworms, ghostly fish, and strange shrimp with eyes on their backs. There are species who live so deep in parts of the ocean that there is absolutely no light, and some of these species have developed a way to illuminate their surroundings by an incandescent light (bioluminescence) they give off from their bodies.

We have done much to begin exploring worlds beyond Earth, first by orbiting the planet and then by our trips to the moon. We have sent many probes to celestial bodies and have landed on these distant worlds. The more recent probes are beginning to sample the atmosphere and analyze the soil. We have perfected satellites that are measuring things around our sun and the planets and are discovering things that we never knew before. *Deep Space 1* (launched October 24, 1998) went into solar orbit. *Voyager 1* (September 5, 1977) and *Voyager 2* (October 20, 1977) were sent out in space. *Cassini* (October 15, 1997) was sent to orbit Saturn, and *Messenger* (August 3, 2004) circles Mercury. *Viking 1* (August 20, 1975) was the first spacecraft to land on Mars. On July 30, 2020, we launched the Mars 2020 *Perseverance* Rover that will land on February 18, 2021. The United States, China, and Russia have successfully landed unmanned spacecraft on the moon.

Mars 2020 *Perseverance* Rover (photo courtesy of NASA)

On January 3, 2019, the Chinese landed their rover, *Yutu-2*, on the far side of the moon. As it was exploring the moon, its camera spotted something glittering in the dust at the bottom of a large crater. Everything on the moon is covered by a gray dust, and something glittering was out of place. The Chinese had their rover go into the crater and examine this object. What they found looked like a gemstone, which scientists believe was created by the extreme heat of a meteor as it struck the moon, causing the crater. Although this discovery does not indicate alien presence on the far side of our moon, it does show the extreme interest of countries on Earth about what might be discovered and the secrets that the moon holds.

We have developed and put into place the Hubble Space Telescope (launched April 24, 1990), which has produced some of the most astounding pictures and greater insight into the development of our universe and Earth itself. It has enabled astronomers to look back billions of years. The pictures we are seeing today from the Hubble telescope depict our universe as it existed as long as 13.5 billion years ago. These pictures travel across space at the speed of 186,000 miles per second (the speed of light). The distance, for example, between New York City and London is approximately 3,500 miles. This means that light would make 53 trips from New York to London every second. In one year, there are just over 31.5 million seconds. Now imagine a trip that took 13.5 billion years and you get some idea of the enormity of our universe.

In 2021, we expect to put into place the successor to the Hubble telescope, the James Webb Space Telescope. The technology employed in the Webb telescope is light-years ahead of what exists in the Hubble.[1] What mysteries that instrument will help solve is conjecture at this point, but fascinating. In May 2020, NASA announced the next and even more powerful space telescope, named after Nancy Grace Roman, NASA's first chief astronomer and woman executive. It is expected to be in orbit by the mid-2020s.[2]

In addition to the extensive studies that are being done about the formation of the earth and our universe using instruments such as the Hubble telescope, a great deal of work has been done by some of the most prestigious scientists on Earth to understand our history.

One line of thought postulates that intelligent and advanced civilizations existed on Earth far before what our current doctrine acknowledges. This idea says civilizations existed on Earth in our distant past, as much as one hundred thousand or more years ago. Evidence is being uncovered that shows intelligent civilizations may have existed in areas such as Mesopotamia, Samaria, Egypt, and Africa. A lost civilization has been found in the Amazon, which predates the Incas. This body of scientists believes these life-forms disappeared for some unexplained reason and much later intelligent beings developed and are what we have acknowledged as our ancestors, dating back to about 4000 BC. Some contend that these much earlier life-forms originated on Earth, while others propose they may have been of extraterrestrial origin.

There are very different opinions among experts as to the age of the Great Egyptian Sphinx. Two Ukrainian researchers believe that the Sphinx could be as much as eight hundred thousand years old, which would be a revolutionary discovery. The two scientists who support this theory are Vjacheslav Manichev and Alexander Parkhomenko, of the National Academy of Sciences of Ukraine. Their theories differ greatly from the Egyptologists who believe the Sphinx was built about 2500 BC.

Recent studies have shown, for example, it is possible to move the huge stones used to build the Pyramids over extended distances by mounting them on a sled and pouring water in front of the sled. This significantly reduces the friction between the sled and the sand, which enables the movement of extremely heavy objects such as the stones used to build the Pyramids. The next time you go to the shore pull something through the dry sand and then pull the same thing along the water's edge on wet sand, and you will see how much easier it is to pull something on wet sand.

It has also been discovered that the precision of some of the stones in the Pyramids is not as precise as some have claimed. In fact, there are gaps between many of the stones, some of which have been filled with a type of mortar that was made by burning limestone. They have been able to carbon date the wood that was used to burn the limestone and confirm that the Pyramids were probably made about 2500 BC. These most recent studies confirm the original belief by Egyptologists as to their origin. That, however, does not carry forward to the age of the Sphinx itself, which is still a huge mystery.

The studies that were done on elongated skulls found in Peru are especially intriguing. Their discovery is significant and will be more fully covered later. The extent scientists have gone to investigate the possibility of extraterrestrial life visiting Earth in our distant past is substantial. It took five years to analyze the DNA from the teeth in the elongated skulls to determine that they were not from this planet.

Beginning in 1947 with the reported crash of an alien spacecraft at Roswell, New Mexico, the attention of people on Earth turned to the question, What, if anything, is out there? Since Roswell, literally tens of thousands of sightings have been reported that seem to indicate that spacecraft, unlike anything on Earth, have been appearing all over the world. Some of the sightings are received with skepticism, some are pure fabrication, while others are very difficult to debunk. Radar confirmation and observations by experienced pilots and other highly trained individuals increase the credibility of many of these sightings. In addition, the volume of these sightings and their appearance over populated areas have significantly increased during the past several decades.

The purpose of this book is to look at some of the information published about the possible existence of intelligent life out there and whether they have been visiting our planet. It is impossible to list the tens of thousands of individual pieces of information published, and even if one could, it would become very boring. What I have chosen to do is to provide samples of some of the reported incidents and let the reader decide what to accept and what to reject. In conclusion, I will review what I believe to be the most important sightings and provide the reader with my military analysis of the issues we could face from extraterrestrial life.

1

Human Curiosity

During the last several decades and especially in the last ten years, scientists all over the world have been looking at our past, looking at the stars, and trying to answer the question, Does extraterrestrial life exist? They have employed a process called the scientific method, which is the outline of how scientists go about studying various issues. The scientific method consists of the following steps:

- Make an observation.
- Ask a question.
- Form a hypothesis.
- Make a prediction.
- Test the prediction.
- Use the results to make a new prediction.

In order to conduct these studies to uncover the mysteries they are investigating, scientists use some of the most up-to-date techniques. Some of the technologies being employed include carbon dating, DNA analysis, and the use of MRIs and other imaging equipment.

Carbon dating, for example, enables us to establish the age of organic material such as plants and animals. In recent years, the development of more sensitive and accurate instruments has improved the ability to date living things. All plants and animals contain carbon. Of the three types of carbon, which are called isotopes, one is called carbon-14. This isotope of carbon declines at a constant pace, and by measuring the amount of carbon-14 that remains in a living organism, we can determine its age. In the past we were able to go back as much as twenty-five thousand years, but with the development of improved accelerator mass spectrometers, science has been able to go back an astounding fifty thousand years. At the point of fifty thousand years most of the carbon-14 has disintegrated, and therefore it is not possible to date something beyond that time.

DNA is another term that we have all become familiar with in the past few years. The use of computers and increased technology have enabled us to use DNA as a common tool to identify individuals to trace our lineage and to determine the differences that exist between different species of life on Earth. One of the most fascinating things we have learned by studying DNA is that many living things have a great deal of DNA that is very similar. For example, the similarity in the DNA between one human being and another is 99.9 percent. Therefore, the difference in the DNA between you and your child is only one-tenth of 1 percent.

As astounding as this fact is, scientists compared the similarity of human DNA with other living things with the following results:

- Chimpanzee: 96% similar
- Mice: 85% similar
- Cow: 80% similar
- Fruit fly: 61% similar
- Chicken: 60% similar
- Banana: 60% similar

One of the most effective ways scientists have developed to examine DNA in animals from the past is by removing dentine from the center of their teeth. As it turns out, the enamel is almost a perfect protective covering for the dentine in the center of the tooth, which contains DNA material. This was one of the techniques used to examine the elongated skulls discovered in Peru. In May of this past year, the results of a five-year-long analysis of the DNA that was examined from the teeth in these skulls determined that they were **not of this earth**. Even though the scientists concluded that the DNA was unlike anything on Earth, it still did contain the basic structure of DNA.

Scientists are also using sophisticated imaging devices to look through mummies and other artifacts to get a better idea of their structure and internal configuration. This was also true on the elongated skulls, where they were searching for the sagittal sutures, which are present on the top of all human skulls. They employed MRI scans on the skulls but were unable to locate these sutures on the elongated skulls, which is further indication that they are not simply another species of humanoids.

The news is full of exploration—looking at our past, trying to figure out our future, and attempting to understand where we came from and whether or not we are truly alone in this universe. Every week, we see stories about exploration that show what archaeologists are doing. Some of this work is enlightening and raises some very real issues about our past. For example, the mystery surrounding the age of the Sphinx has been of interest for a long time. When was it was made and who made it?

Conventional thought is that the Sphinx was made about 2500 BC. Recent studies claim that at least part of the erosion of the Sphinx is not the result of wind or dust but rather the effects of water. This challenges the origin and age of the Sphinx because there was no water at its location in 2500 BC. In addition, it would take a long time for erosion to take place. The proponents of this theory suggest that the Sphinx is much older than we have been taught. They contend civilization is far more distant in time than we first believed. Robert Schoch, a geologist and an associate professor of natural sciences at Boston University, proposed one such theory. He concluded that the weathering of the Sphinx was caused by prolonged and extensive rainfall. He therefore concluded that the Sphinx was constructed about 6000 BC. However, most experts and Egyptologists have provided alternative rationale for the erosion, and the belief by the preponderance of scientists is that the Sphinx was created when originally thought—about 2500 BC.[3]

Another issue associated with Egypt and our history is the Pyramids. Many questions remain unanswered and get to the point of whether or not we may have had help in their design and construction. Certain facts are very clear: pyramids exist all over the world and their orientation is the same regardless of where the pyramid was constructed. This begs the question of how different societies could create the same type of structure with the identical orientation without some sort of central direction.

In addition to this question, we have the more pragmatic issue of how ancient civilizations, without the use of modern machinery, would have been able to cut stones with such precision, move them to the construction sites, and build such massive structures not only in Egypt but also all over the world, although, as noted in the introduction, the question of precision may have been answered. Much speculation continues that the pyramids had some specific purpose and were constructed with the help of extraterrestrial beings. Although there is certainly no definitive answer to this question, it is difficult to explain how they were made, why they are similar in design, and how they can be oriented exactly the same no matter where they are located. According to the website Mysterious Unexplained History, there are thousands of pyramids all over the world. This website documents most of the known pyramids, and what they document is astounding.

Another supposed artifact that begs the question of how far back the history of man goes is the London Hammer, located in Glen Rose, Texas. The owner has speculated that, based on the wooden handle and its condition, the iron hammer is over 140 million years old. If true, that would then raise the question: How could we have a tool that old when the history of humanoids using tools only goes back about forty thousand years?[4] Analysis done on this hammer revealed that the iron itself was probably similar to iron that was made two hundred years ago.

Analysis on the wooden handle was not allowed by the owner to verify, using carbon dating, whether the handle was in fact more than two hundred years old. A detailed analysis of this hammer by the Creation Evidence Museum indicates that in fact this is not a hammer that dates back 140 million years but rather an artifact from about two hundred years ago. It is important in looking at any of these developments to make sure that we really do apply the best science and information so we do not jump to conclusions that may take us down the wrong path.

Man has always wondered about the heavens. The first telescope to look at the sky was invented by Dutch eyeglass maker Hans Lippershey in 1608.[5] Galileo made his first telescope about the same time. He studied the skies and observed the planets. He published *The Starry Messenger* in 1610 and reported on the moon, Jupiter, and the Milky Way. Galileo drew pictures of the phases of the moon, and his observations helped convince scientists of what Copernicus proposed in 1543—that the earth revolves around the sun. Galileo's first telescope initially magnified approximately eight times, and later he enhanced it to twenty times. That is very different from what we have today in telescopes like the Hubble. It was, however, the beginning of modern astronomy and looking into the origins of our planet and the universe.[6]

Other interesting phenomena are the many drawings and carvings that appear from our past. Some seem to indicate that aliens may have visited our ancestors. It is certainly true that people, going back thousands of years, drew and carved what they saw on walls in caves and in temples. Some of these images appear to look like beings in the sky. We have also found that hereto fakery has been attempted. What comes to mind is a carving that looks like an astronaut in his spacesuit on a cathedral in Salamanca, Spain. It was carved on a doorway of a cathedral built in the early twelfth century to make it look as though it were part of the original construction. It was discovered that a worker added the astronaut carving in 1992 while restoring the cathedral. Nevertheless, some of the pictures and carvings that we see throughout the world are authentic and do look like alien creatures coming from the sky.[7]

Carving of astronaut on cathedral in Salamanca, Spain.

Worker restoring the building added it in 1992.
(photo from iStock by Getty Images)

Below are examples of ancient depictions of what appear to be aliens. (photos from iStock by Getty Images)

Now that we have looked at some of the evidence beginning with prehistoric times up through the Pyramids in Egypt, it is time to look at evidence that is more recent. Roswell was the event that triggered the interest of scientists, governments, and the public as to the possibility of intelligent life elsewhere in the universe. This interest has continued to grow as the number of sightings has increased.

2

Roswell, July 3, 1947

The incident that is reported to have occurred at Roswell, New Mexico, on July 4, 1947, captured the imagination of many people and really accelerated the discussion about UFOs and extraterrestrial beings. I have always been curious about Roswell, but I chose to write this book because of the increased sightings as well as a recent acknowledgment by our Department of Defense.

Col. Philip Corso's book, *The Day After Roswell*, contains a lot of information, which I have taken the time to try to verify from other sources. I have researched the incidents and the people that he mentions in his book, including Majestic 12, and in every case, what Colonel Corso has claimed in his book with respect to these individuals appears to be accurate. In addition, much of what the colonel included in his book is also included in the History Channel source I have cited. It should be noted that Colonel Corso himself was not physically present at Roswell in July 1947, but he did interview others who were there at that time.

In 1947 the US Army operated two major sites, the White Sands Missile Range and Alamogordo near Roswell, New Mexico. At White Sands, they were testing V2 rockets that had been captured from the Germans after World War II, while at Alamogordo nuclear testing was being done. These installations were extremely sensitive and subject to scrutiny by the intelligence networks of our army and air force.

In the period leading up to July 4, a series of severe lightning storms took place at White Sands. In addition, radar began to show a number of blips, which began to increase at an alarming rate. Because of this unusual activity, the army's Counter Intelligence Corps (CIC) sent some of its best agents to White Sands. The fear at the time was that the Russians might have been spying on these two sensitive facilities in New Mexico. There was some thought that they may have snuck under our radar through either Canada or Mexico, and the Pentagon was greatly concerned about this activity.

The numerous radar sightings showed that the objects on the screen were able to travel at speeds that no known aircraft could achieve. The blips went from almost stationary to between 1,000 and 2,000 miles per hour in approximately one second. Not only was it impossible for any known aircraft to accelerate at that rate, but if an aircraft had been able to accelerate at anything close to that rate, the pilots would have died because of the extreme g-force that would have resulted.

Though there is a bit of confusion regarding the exact date, on either the second or the third of July 1947, during a thunderstorm, the 509th Bomb Group of the Eighth Air Force, stationed at White Sands, observed a blip on the screen that darted rapidly across the radar display. All of a sudden, there was a violent explosion that produced a brilliant white fluorescent light about eight to ten miles from the base, and at that moment, the blip on the screen disappeared.

This explosion was seen on the other side of the site by the townspeople in Roswell. In particular, the sheriff's and fire departments observed this flash of light on the horizon. They were about the same distance from the explosion as the military at White Sands.

The CIC at White Sands immediately mobilized, and the base commander, Col. William Blanchard, was notified of the incident. The analysis was that something had crashed and caused the explosion that was clearly seen both on the base and in the town of Roswell. Colonel Blanchard immediately dispatched the CIC team with a full recovery complement that included trucks, a flatbed, and a crane in the direction of the explosion. In addition to the CIC, a full complement of MPs was dispatched to the site.

The sheriff's and fire departments also sent contingents toward the flash, not knowing that the military was on its way from the opposite side of the crash. The military contingent arrived just before the contingent from Roswell. The military police immediately began to cordon off the area and directed the Roswell Fire and Police Departments to not cross the line and approach the crash site. However, one member of the fire department did locate debris from what appeared to be a crash site and pick up a piece of cloth that he put in his pocket without the knowledge of the military.

From eyewitness accounts, there was a saucerlike craft partially in the ground with a large crack in its structure. There were three dead humanoid figures at the crash site. Another such creature appeared to be badly injured and was crawling out of the crack in the vessel. A fifth was running away from the site. A military police member shouted at the figure running away from the site to halt, and when it did not stop he shot and killed the creature with his M1 rifle.

The recovery team immediately began the process of picking up all the debris at the crash site. They covered the five dead aliens and put them in the trucks along with all the other debris, and the crane lifted the aircraft onto the flatbed truck. They covered the aircraft with a tarpaulin, and everything was taken to White Sands. The military informed the Roswell Sheriff's and Fire Departments to disregard anything they had seen and not to discuss the matter with anyone.[8]

Shortly after the incident Lydia Sleppy, who worked for KOAT radio in Brunswick, New Mexico, received a call from John McBoil, the regional general manager of the radio station, informing her that a flying saucer had crashed at Roswell. Soon after receiving the call from McBoil, Mrs. Sleppy got a message from the FBI directing her to stop all communications regarding this incident.[9] In addition, on July 8, the *Roswell Daily Record*, a local newspaper, ran the story on the front page.

The Pentagon was so concerned that they immediately dispatched Lt. Gen. Nathan Twining to Roswell to investigate the incident.[10] Because of General Twining's visit, Gen. Roger Remy was directed to create a cover story to explain the incident. Lt. Walter Haut was told to fabricate a story that a weather balloon had crashed near Roswell as an explanation for the incident.[11] On June 30, 2007, former Lieutenant Haut made a deathbed confession acknowledging that a spacecraft did crash at Roswell and that he had been directed to create the cover story about the weather balloon.[12] Thirty years after the incident, a retired Maj. Jesse Maxwell, who was at Roswell when the crash occurred, came forward and admitted that the crash did in fact occur and that he had been directed to cover up the incident. Maxwell claims, at the time of the crash, he saw the debris from the ship, the ship itself, and dead aliens moved into an autopsy facility at White Sands, New Mexico. Maxwell also claims that some of the debris removed from the crash site remained at White Sands along with two of the dead aliens. The ship and three of the other dead aliens were transported to Wright-Patterson Air Force Base.

In 1955, a US Air Force technician by the name of Norma Gardner was stationed at Wright-Patterson Air Force Base. Her job was to catalog items taken from alien crashes. She cataloged more than one thousand items from UFO crashes but was sworn to secrecy about what she saw. Airman Gardner, on her deathbed, said, "the government [could] no longer keep [her] from telling the truth," and she explained that not only had she cataloged unidentified items from alien crash sites but that she personally saw four-foot gray beings in tanks at Wright-Patterson Air Force Base. She also claimed there were autopsy reports from the gray beings.[13] The term "Grays" can be traced back to the reported crash at Roswell in 1947.

The incident at Roswell was brought to the attention of President Harry Truman. He authorized the Secretary of Defense, James Forrestal, to establish a supersecret group with the codename Majestic 12. He further directed Secretary Forrestal to have all external discussions with the office of the president only.[14]

The original twelve members of Majestic 12
Who were the men that were entrusted with the most important secrets in history?

Vice Adm. Roscoe H. Hillenkoetter: the first director of the Central Intelligence Agency.

Vannevar Bush: the engineer who marshaled American technology for World War II and ushered in the Atomic Age.

James V. Forrestal: secretary of the navy and the first United States secretary of defense.

Gen. Nathan Twining: chief of staff of the United States Air Force from 1953 until 1957 and chairman of the Joint Chiefs of Staff from 1957 to 1960.

Gen. Hoyt S. Vandenberg: the **second chief of staff of the US Air Force.**

Detlev Wulf Bronk: a prominent American scientist, educator, and administrator credited with establishing biophysics as a recognized discipline.

Dr. Jerome C. Hunsaker: an aviation pioneer who founded the first college course in aeronautical engineering at the Massachusetts Institute of Technology.

Sidney William Souers: an American admiral and intelligence expert who was appointed as the first director of central intelligence on January 23, 1946, by President Harry S. Truman.

Gordon Gray: an official in the government of the United States during the administrations of Harry Truman and Dwight Eisenhower who was associated with defense and national security.

Donald Howard Menzel: one of the first theoretical astronomers and astrophysicists in the United States.

Robert Miller Montague: a lieutenant general in the United States Army who achieved prominence as the deputy commander of Fort Bliss, Texas, and commander of the Sandia Missile Base in New Mexico.

Lloyd Viel Berkner: an American physicist and engineer who was one of the inventors of the measuring device that since has become standard at ionosphere stations because it measures the height and electron density of the ionosphere.

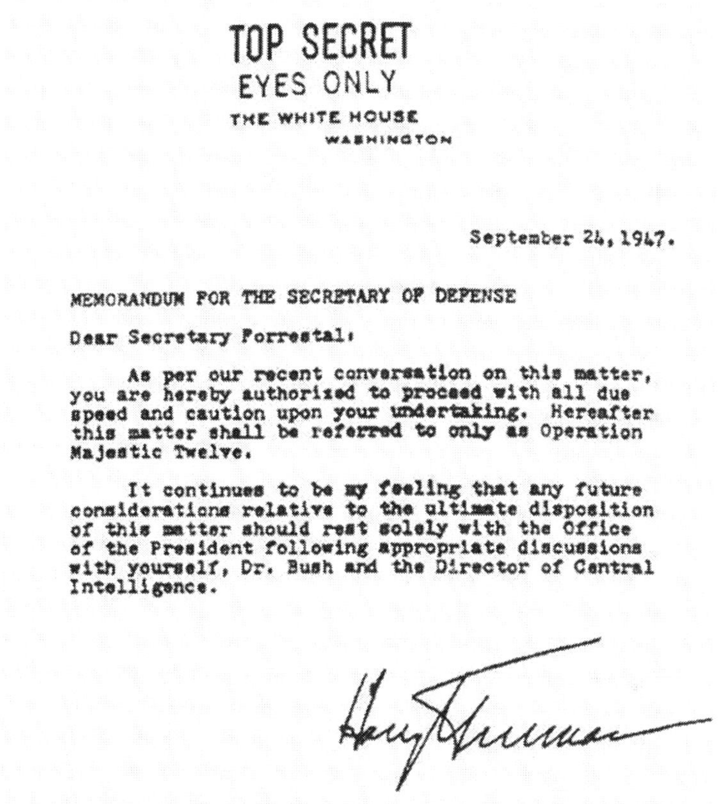

TOP SECRET
EYES ONLY
THE WHITE HOUSE
WASHINGTON

September 24, 1947.

MEMORANDUM FOR THE SECRETARY OF DEFENSE

Dear Secretary Forrestal:

As per our recent conversation on this matter, you are hereby authorized to proceed with all due speed and caution upon your undertaking. Hereafter this matter shall be referred to only as Operation Majestic Twelve.

It continues to be my feeling that any future considerations relative to the ultimate disposition of this matter should rest solely with the Office of the President following appropriate discussions with yourself, Dr. Bush and the Director of Central Intelligence.

Harry Truman

The letter sent to Secretary Forrestal by President Truman authorizing the establishment of this supersecret group.
(image courtesy of www.mufor.org)

The urgency that President Truman placed on the crash at Roswell was evident by the fact that reports circulated that Secretary Forrestal himself went to Roswell. These reports also indicated that Secretary Forrestal was in fact present during autopsies that were performed on the dead aliens at White Sands. After his visit to Roswell, there was a marked change in James Forrestal's behavior, and two years later he resigned as secretary of defense. Soon after, his physical and mental conditions deteriorated, and he was placed in a naval hospital for approximately a month. His brother finally demanded his brother be released from the hospital and informed officials that he was going to the hospital the following day to remove him. That night, James Forrestal either was pushed or jumped out of a sixteen-story hospital window to his death.

After the creation of Majestic 12 and the absolute secrecy with which this group operated, Forrestal, as a member of the group, believed that the public had a right to know what was being discussed with respect to extraterrestrial life and alien visits to our planet. He was at odds with the other members of Majestic 12, and many believe that James Forrestal's condition and the likelihood that he might reveal the details behind Roswell are the reason for his death. The secretary believed unidentified individuals dressed in black clothing were following him. There is no definitive proof that the secretary was in fact murdered. His strange behavior after his visit to Roswell, his unexpected resignation, the deterioration of his mental condition, and the fact that he was at odds with the other members of Majestic 12 regarding the secrecy of what they were doing do lend themselves to some serious questioning as to his death. Since his death occurred in a naval hospital, the US Navy immediately declared that his death was a suicide. There was no further investigation into the secretary's death until scuff marks were discovered on the floor at the window where he fell. Again, nothing resulted from that revelation.[15]

We fast-forward to 1961 when then Lt. Col. Philip Corso was assigned to head the Foreign Technology Desk in the office of Army Research and Development at the Pentagon. Prior to that time, the colonel had served on General MacArthur's staff in Korea and later on the National Security Council during the administration of Dwight Eisenhower, whom he knew personally. As head of the Foreign

Technology Desk, Lieutenant Colonel Corso reported directly to the chief of the Army Research and Development office in the Pentagon, Lt. Gen. Arthur G. Trudeau. Lieutenant Colonel Corso served in that office from 1961 to 1963. After retirement as a colonel, he went to work on the staffs of Senators James Eastland and Strom Thurmond, specializing in national security.

Corso had heard a lot about Roswell and the stories about the highly secret materials that were uncovered at the crash site. He had no personal knowledge and was not at Roswell in July 1947, but his new assignment at the Pentagon, according to the account in his book, *The Day After Roswell*, would put a very new light on the Roswell story.

Upon assignment to the Pentagon, General Trudeau called Lieutenant Colonel Corso into his office and told him that he would be given the file drawer located in the corner of the general's office. It would be his responsibility to oversee and utilize the information in that container. The general did not go into detail, and that day the filing cabinet was relocated from the general's office to Colonel Corso's office, one floor below. The colonel was somewhat surprised and finally began the process of looking into what the general had provided in that locked file cabinet.[16] To say the least, the colonel was astounded at what he found. One of the first things he came upon was a report that described in excruciating detail the autopsies that had been performed on alien bodies retrieved from the crash site at Roswell in 1947. These clearly were medical reports that contained detailed information as to the physiology and structure of the bodies.[17]

They were described as approximately four and a half feet tall with large heads and eyes. Their color was a gray tone, and the texture of their skin was like that of a dolphin. Their internal organs were different from humans, and their bones were stronger than human bones and much more flexible. The descriptions, in medical terms, of the structure of these gray humanoids was very detailed.[18]

In looking through the filing cabinet, the colonel found

- cloth that looked like nothing he had ever seen before;
- a device that looked like a handheld laser of today;
- a band that looked as if it apparently went around the head of the aliens;
- filaments that looked like what today we call fiber-optic strands;
- a piece of what looked like a circuit board in a modern-day computer; and
- a thin film that when held up to the eye made it look as if it were daytime in the dark.[19]

After the colonel had gone through the material in the filing cabinet, he realized that what he had been given were elements that had been taken from the Roswell crash site in 1947 and then safeguarded for fourteen years. The general ask Corso to report to him in his office, and they began discussing what had been preserved and stored in this safe-like container.

It was at that point that Lieutenant Colonel Corso was informed that his job would be to develop a plan to utilize this information and material. He was to work with the contractors that were producing the most sophisticated and highly classified weapons for the military and to provide this material to them. The intent was for the contractors to reverse engineer this technology and use it to develop weapons and other things that would be useful to the military. The general explained that the way he wanted Corso to go about this was to provide the information and items to the appropriate contractors with existing contracts so that it would not raise suspicion. There was a significant concern about such information getting into the hands of the Russians, and the general did not trust other agencies like the FBI and CIA.

J. Edgar Hoover, the FBI director, was very interested in stories about Roswell. As it turned out, Colonel Corso and the director developed a relationship. The colonel provided Mr. Hoover with information about Roswell, and the director looked into the background of individuals and contractors that the colonel wanted to approach for using the Roswell material.

The colonel proceeded to review the contractors and the projects they were working on to try to associate the items that he had in his possession from Roswell with their current work on weapons systems. One example was integrated circuits and the thin filaments of glass that later turned out to be fiber optics. We had existing contracts with companies like Bell Labs and IBM, and they were provided with the circuitry and the fiber optics. Over the next two years, Corso worked with our defense contractors to provide them with the knowledge and technology that he had received from the general. According to Colonel Corso, these efforts resulted in either the development of or the acceleration of the development for the following:

- Integrated circuits
- Kevlar vests (from the fabric they found on the aliens' bodies)
- Focused energy weapons (accelerated particle beams)
- Lasers
- Night-vision technology
- Fiber optics
- Mind-control devices[20]

One of the most fascinating things taken from the craft was the bands that, when put around your head, created a strange mental reaction. These bands were later determined to be the way in which the alien pilots controlled their spacecraft. This technology just today is being incorporated into the helmets of the pilots for the F-35. At the time of the crash, a decision was made to take three alien bodies and the spacecraft to Wright-Patterson Air Force Base, and the colonel had no direct knowledge of what the air force was doing with the spacecraft itself or any developments that might have resulted from the technology they discovered by reverse engineering the craft.

One of the areas of research was creating aircraft that could defy gravity, similar to the experiments that were being done by the Germans at the end of World War II. The feeling was that the alien spacecraft that crashed at Roswell operated by creating its own gravitational field, which not only was able to propel the spacecraft but also protected the pilots from the extreme g-force that would result from the extreme rate of acceleration.

From the discussions between General Trudeau and Colonel Corso, it became clear that the real objective—to reverse engineer and use the technology from Roswell to accelerate our technological development—was intended not only to defend ourselves against countries like Russia but also to effectively deal with aliens whose purpose might be something other than observation. Clearly, these visitors from outside our planet possessed knowledge and a level of technology far superior to what we had developed. The focused energy beams and lasers that were later developed are two of the types of weapons systems that might prove effective against alien spacecraft. The development of integrated circuits, Kevlar, and many other things, if in fact what Colonel Corso stated in his book was accurate, has moved our technology forward at a more rapid pace.

Another area of speculation is whether our enemies on Earth have similar technology from crashes that may have occurred in their territory. It is unknown if our intelligence officials are aware of alien technology that may be in the hands of other countries.

One thing is clear: the level of knowledge and technology that would be necessary to move in space, as the aliens appeared to accomplish, is far beyond that which we currently possess.

Although some may look at the information contained in Colonel Corso's book as fabricated or possibly exaggerated, from my research, every one of the individuals he identified in his book not only existed but also were as the colonel described. The deathbed declarations of the air force woman at Wright-Patterson Air Force Base who cataloged more than one thousand artifacts from crash sites and claims she saw

alien bodies is important. The deathbed statement of the public rela-
tions officer at Roswell who admits he not only fabricated the balloon
story but also that he saw the spacecraft and the alien bodies does make
it much harder to discount the claims in Colonel Corso's book.

In addition, there is a four-page list of witnesses at Roswell that
is reported in the book *UFO Crash at Roswell*, by Kevin Randle and
Donald Schmitt.[21]

The reader will have to evaluate for himself or herself the truth of
everything that is included in the colonel's book as well as the material
presented in the History Channel special *UFO Conspiracy: Hunt for the
Truth*. Both of the sources are in agreement with each other and were
used in the above discussion of Roswell.

3

Sightings after Roswell

If the incident at Roswell had been the only experience, the interest in extraterrestrials would have most likely faded away. That, however, was simply not the case as many other sightings began taking place in the United States and in other countries of the world. Below is a sample of some of those sightings, which shows why the interest of both our government and the public has been growing. Because of these increased observations, many scientists, apart from the government, have become interested in investigating UFO sightings. A number of organizations have expended a great deal of time, energy, and money to document and analyze the many sightings that have occurred. Some of the most notable are shown below.

March 1951

Project BLUE BOOK was authorized by Gen. Nathan F. Twining and headed by Capt. Edward Ruppelt. The stated objectives of Project BLUE BOOK were to determine if UFOs were a threat to our security and to scientifically analyze UFO-related data.

The project lasted until the end of 1969 and collected 12,618 UFO reports. The conclusion was that most of the reports were misidentifications of natural phenomena or conventional aircraft sightings.[22]

Many people, after looking at what Project BLUE BOOK did, have concluded that the real purpose of this air force activity was to discredit UFO sightings. Certainly, some of the sightings are misidentifications and some may be sightings of futuristic weapons that we are in the process of developing. One legitimate question about the sighting of futuristic weapons is, If they are so secret, would not our military limit any such test flights to areas where people would most likely not observe them? When you look more deeply into some of the incidents that were reported and compare them to the rationale that Project BLUE BOOK assigned to that incident, it does add credibility to the idea that a cover-up was the real objective of this project.

A number of the sightings between its initiation and the end of 1969 were incidents that were seen by large numbers of individuals, some of whom were highly trained observers, like police officers and pilots, who are trained to provide accurate and detailed assessments of any given situation. Photographs and radar backed up some of these sightings. Any thinking person would challenge the credibility of explanations such as flying birds, lighthouses, or swamp gas. When you ascribe sightings of UFOs to birds and watch the speed with which those objects moved, even a person with a very low IQ would conclude, that simply is not true.

Recently the Department of Defense has acknowledged contact with UFOs and that the DOD has been studying these sightings for some time. There is a great deal of renewed interest in UFO sightings, which I hope will spark an unbiased evaluation of what is taking place. The most significant step in that direction was the acknowledgment, published July 27–29, 2020, that the US Navy has had contact with UFOs. If we could look into the classified files of the investigations that have been going on for the last ten years, we would likely find evidence of many more encounters, especially with our military. We can only hope that this renewed effort to get to the truth will produce some answers about intelligent life visiting our planet.

August 25, 1951

Three scientists from Texas Tech, in Lubbock, Texas, saw twenty-five to thirty lights across the sky. They saw a second group in the same area and contacted the US Air Force. The objects continued to appear until September 1951.[23]

August 30, 1951

Carl Hart Jr., a student in Lubbock, Texas, took two photographs of an unidentified flying object. He later provided the pictures to the US Air Force, which ended up in Project BLUE BOOK. The air force claims they were reflections from streetlights of some birds that flew by. The problem was that the speed with which these objects moved far exceeded anything a bird could fly.[24]

1955

Norma Gardner, an airman stationed at Wright-Patterson Air Force Base, cataloged over one thousand items taken from alien crash sites. She claimed to have seen four-foot gray aliens in tanks filled with preservative and later made a deathbed statement about her experience.[25]

November 2, 1957

In Levelland, Texas, hundreds of people claimed they saw alien spacecraft over a road, actually blocking the highway. The sheriff claims that the spacecraft were cigar shaped and informed the US Air Force. A sergeant from Project BLUE BOOK was sent to Levelland. Upon investigation, the air force said it was due to a storm, but at the time of the sightings there was no storm recorded in the area. There were rumors that the real intent of Project BLUE BOOK was to discredit UFO sightings rather than to investigate them.[26]

December 9, 1965

The FAA tracked the flight path of unidentified objects, which were verified by twenty-three pilots. On December 9, 1965, there was a crash in the woods at Kecksburg, Pennsylvania. People from the town found the aircraft, which was said to be a saucer shape with windows on the side. John Murphy, of radio station WHJB in Greensburg, Pennsylvania, reported the crash. The military arrived, directed the people to leave the site, and took John Murphy's notes. A large flatbed truck was brought to the site and removed the aircraft.

Later, the government denied that there was any aircraft and said it was a meteor despite the fact that there were hundreds of witnesses from the town. John Murphy interviewed all of the witnesses and planned to present what he had learned on a radio show. Several men in black approached him and convinced him not to air the show about the UFO. The men took all of John Murphy's notes and recordings from him.

In 1967 Murphy decided to reopen his investigation, and two days after he made the announcement, he was killed by a hit-and-run driver who was never found.[27]

1966

Computer missile specialist JK claims that he saw nine alien bodies stored in glass containers in an underground vault at Wright-Patterson Air Force Base.[28]

1966

Barry Goldwater was interested in the Roswell story and the items stored at Wright-Patterson Air Force Base. He asked his close friend Gen. Curtis LeMay about the aliens and what was being stored at Wright-Patterson. For the only time in his life, his friend General LeMay told Barry Goldwater never to talk about that to him again.

Skeptics should take a look on YouTube at an interview with Barry Goldwater that was posted April 2, 2009, by Paul Robinson. Barry Goldwater directly explains on camera that he had a conversation with Gen. Curtis LeMay, with whom he was a very close friend, about UFO material being stored at Wright-Patterson Air Force Base. In that interview, Mr. Goldwater relayed that General LeMay became very angry with him when he asked that question. He told him not to speak of it again. That certainly is a very strange response from a friend to a matter-of-fact question.[29]

March 14, 1966

In Washtenaw County, Michigan, most of a town saw UFOs, including two sheriff's officers, Buford Bushroe and John Foster. The officers reported seeing the objects move at fantastic speeds. The sightings continued for about a week, and on March 20 a spacecraft landed in a swamp. Sheriff's deputies reported the spacecraft to the US Air Force, and after investigating, the air force claimed it was due to swamp gas.

There were so many reports of the UFOs in Michigan that then-congressman Gerald Ford demanded a hearing to look into the sightings.[30]

March 16, 1967

On March 16, 1967, at approximately 0845, ten Minuteman missiles of the Maelstrom Air Force Base went off-line. At the same time, security personnel at the base said there were UFOs sighted overhead. It took approximately twenty-four hours to restore the missiles to "ready status." After an extensive evaluation by the air force, no conclusive reason for this incident was determined. A similar incident took place at another Minuteman site during the same period. There was no direct correlation between the sightings of the UFOs and what took place at these two Minuteman sites, but the details surrounding both incidents were very similar. These incidents were recorded in the 341st Special Missile Wing history.[31]

June 15, 1968

On June 15, 1968, on the river near Cua Viet, Vietnam, at approximately 12:30 a.m., two US Navy patrol boats, one commanded by Lieutenant Davis and the other by Lieutenant Snyder, saw two flying saucers hovering over the river in front of them. The patrol boat commanded by Lieutenant Davis exploded and was destroyed, and the two UFOs disappeared. Lieutenant Snyder was ordered to continue moving up the river. Two UFOs appeared again, and Lieutenant Snyder began to fire at them. Immediately, the same kind of fire that he was using against the UFOs was returned at his patrol boat. Snyder decided to turn around and head toward the open sea where an Australian ship, the *Hobart*, was operating. He reported the incident to the navy, who dispatched several F-4s from Da Nang. Lieutenant Snyder was ordered to keep radio silence.

The navy F-4s spotted two UFOs in the ocean over the *Hobart*. They fired air-to-air missiles at the two flying saucers, which immediately departed at a high rate of speed. The description of the two UFOs over the *Hobart* was identical to that of the two flying saucers that had engaged the patrol boats on the river earlier.

The following day, a missile that appeared to come out of nowhere struck the *Hobart* operating at sea. Immediately the crewmen saw two UFOs and the Australian ship received hits from two additional missiles, causing extensive damage. The two alien spacecraft were recorded on radar. When the US Navy examined the damage to the *Hobart*, they found pieces of the missiles that struck the ship, and these fragments contained serial numbers. The navy traced the serial numbers back to one of the missiles that had been fired at the UFOs the preceding day. Apparently, when Lieutenant Snyder fired on the UFOs they somehow captured and returned that same fire. They were also able to capture the air-to-air missiles that were fired at them by the F-4s and use those missiles the next day to attack the *Hobart*.

In its after-action report of this incident the navy concluded that somehow the alien ships were able to turn around the ordinance that was fired at them and use it against our vessels. Because of this after-action report, the DOD issued instructions to both navy and air force pilots not to engage UFOs in the future.[32]

January 6, 1969

One of the most prominent people to have witnessed a UFO sighting is former president Jimmy Carter. The sighting occurred when he was in Leary, Georgia, to give an address to the Lions Club. He and approximately twenty people who were with him saw the UFO above the horizon. On September 18, 1973, he filed a report with the National Investigations Committee on Aerial Phenomena. He was reported to have made a comment that it was the "darndest thing" he had ever seen.

During the 1976 presidential campaign Carter pledged that if he won the presidency, he would seek to have information that the government had released to the public. As it turned out, President Carter was unable to keep his pledge and cited national security concerns as the reason for not releasing the information.[33]

January 18, 1978

During the early morning of January 18, a UFO was sighted flying over Fort Dix and McGuire Air Force Base. An MP on duty saw something at the edge of the runway. It turned out to be a small being with a large head and slender body. The MP panicked, took out his .45, and shot the being several times. It fled over the fence between the two bases.

The MP contacted Sergeant Morris and was told to go to the gate. Sergeant Morris and his colleagues found the alien dead along the runway. They reported that the body had a strong ammonia odor.

Later that day a team from Wright-Patterson Air Force Base arrived in a C-141 cargo aircraft, put the body in a silver-colored box, and took off. Morris and his companions were warned by security not to talk about the incident or they would be court-martialed. Two days later, Morris and the others were taken to Wright-Patterson Air Force Base. They went under extensive interrogation and again were warned not to mention the incident.

Upon return to McGuire, Morris debriefed his commander, and nothing more was said about the incident until many years later. Another witness was Maj. George Filer. The major talked to ABC News, Katelynn Raymer in Washington and David Ruppe in New York. He told these reporters about the alien at the air force base in New Jersey and that the body was found dead after having been shot by one of the airmen on base.[34]

August 1980

A former colonel (name withheld) told Curt Martin that he had seen two live aliens at Wright-Patterson Air Force Base in an underground area. The colonel was dying of cancer and passed away three weeks after the meeting with Martin.[35]

December 27 and 29, 1980

On December 27, 1980, at Bentwaters Royal Air Force Base, a joint base between the United States and Great Britain where nuclear weapons were stored, three enlisted persons saw lights in the sky. They went to what they described as a nine-foot triangle on the ground in Rendlesham Forest. The surface was black with writing on the side that looked like Egyptian hieroglyphics. Staff Sgt. Jim Penniston went to touch the triangle and it immediately disappeared. The lights continued to be visible in the sky.

Two nights later, a report came in of a second sighting. In both cases, the deputy base commander, Lt. Col. Charles Halt, was notified. On the second night, he accompanied several enlisted persons and saw strange lights in the sky. They also found three indentations on the ground in an exact triangle. They made plaster cast molds of the impressions, and it was determined that because of the hardness of the ground, impressions a couple of inches deep could only have been made by a very heavy object. There was a moderate amount of radiation in the three depressions as well as on a tree. Above the area where they saw this triangular craft, the tree branches had been broken as if something had descended from above onto the ground.

The excuse for what they observed on these two dates in December 1980 was that they saw the light from a lighthouse about ten miles away. The eyewitnesses said that was impossible given that the object had moved and left three impressions in the ground.

One of the enlisted men that went to the site on the second night, December 29, 1980, was Airman Larry Warren. He has since come forward and said that not only did he see the craft but he also observed three humanoid-type beings around the spacecraft. Lieutenant Colonel Halt on the second sighting carried with him a tape recorder on which he recorded his observations, and he has that recording today. Halt confirmed he saw the lights and the impressions in the ground but did not see any alien beings at the site. He did say that one of the objects in the sky emitted a beam of light from underneath the craft to the ground.[36]

In mid-August 1956 there had been a report of spacecraft over the same base and authorities dismissed the report.

1983

Mike Reynolds (name changed) met with a retired air force major who worked his entire career at Area 51. The major claimed he was aware that aliens had crashed and that we had reverse engineered some of their technology, and he had written a book about his experience at the base. The major was to be interviewed on the air by Reynolds about his experience. Just prior to the interview, he got a visit from several men in black and the interview was canceled. Reynolds had the major's book in his car and intended to have it published. However, he was approached by two men and told he would not be allowed to publish the book. Mike was shaken up and went into his motel room. When he realized that the book was still in his trunk, he went back out to the car and found that the book was gone. He was again approached by several men and told not to publish the book, or he and his family would be punished. When Mike returned home he found the major would no longer talk with him, and Mike abandoned his plans.

The people who do not believe in the alien existence will discount this account, like many others, but what we are asked to believe is that an air force officer who spent his entire career working at Area 51 was simply making up a story. We also have a reporter who was interested in helping this officer publish his recollections. All of a sudden, both of these people were reportedly contacted by unidentified individuals and threatened. They later decided to abandon the release of the book and the information it contained. If the purpose of the major's book was simply to make a buck and he was not threatened, as he claims, why was his book never published?[37]

November 17, 1986

During Japan Airlines flight 1628 from Reykjavík to Anchorage, at 17:11 over Alaska, the pilot, Capt. Kenju Terauchi, with over thirty thousand air miles of experience, and copilot Terauchi, a former fighter pilot with ten thousand hours in the air, encountered two aircraft to their left. They were going at the same speed as the 747. At 17:18, the two objects veered off and assumed a stack position in front of the airliner. The two craft were flying as if they had overcome gravity. Each object was square shaped. The traffic control at Anchorage could not confirm these aircraft on their short-range radar.

After three minutes, these objects assumed a side-by-side config-uration, which they maintained for another ten minutes, accompanying the airliner. The two craft abruptly left at 17:23, moving to a point below the horizon to the east. The captain used his onboard radar and confirmed that the two craft were approximately seven and a half nautical miles distant. The captain reported that the speed with which the two aircraft had moved and changed directions was like nothing he had ever seen.

As the city lights of Fairbanks began to illuminate objects in the sky, Captain Terauchi noticed a huge spaceship to his left. The object was approximately twice the size of an aircraft carrier and flying at thirty-one thousand feet. The captain executed a 360-degree turn, hoping the gigantic craft would continue forward. However, the aircraft mirrored his turn and continue to shadow the 747. This continued for thirty-one minutes, and the entire sighting lasted approximately fifty minutes.

After Japan flight 1628 arrived safely at Anchorage, the captain filed a formal Federal Aviation Administration report together with the data from his onboard radar and the tapes from the conversation between him and the tower at Anchorage. The data was sent to the Regional Technical Center in Atlantic City, New Jersey, where Vice Adm. Donald Engen reviewed it. John Callahan, the FAA division chief for accidents, saw the material and said it was the first time they had recorded data on a UFO in their possession. After watching the radar images and listening to the audio recordings they were told not to speak of it again and that it "never took place."

The FAA report did reveal that the captain had made other reports of sightings on two separate occasions. On January 29, 1987, at 18:40, Alaskan Airlines flight 50 observed three fast-moving aircraft and through their onboard radar determined that the speed was 3,600 miles per hour.

If this sighting, reported by the pilot with accompanying radar and the voice exchange with the Anchorage tower, is all a lie, why were the recordings and other data confiscated. Why were they told this never took place? If it was all just a hoax and a lot of hot air, it seems hard to understand the reaction of federal officials to force the captain and others to make believe it never happened.[38]

November 29, 1989

Known as the Belgian UFO wave, sightings at eighty locations across Belgium with over one hundred fifty identical reports covered a period of eighteen months. The sightings all reported a triangular craft with three white lights on each of the angles and a red light in the center of the craft.

On April 4, 1990, a picture was taken of the triangular craft. It was sent for an extensive yearlong examination and determined to be genuine.[39] Infrared analysis of the picture taken in Belgium showed that the aircraft was most likely propelled by an electromagnetic system. The aircraft went from speeds of 150 knots to more than 990 knots in less than a second and was confirmed by radar. In England, three years later, they had a series of identical sightings of triangular aircraft with the same lights.[40]

Discounting a single report is one thing; ignoring one hundred fifty reports that are virtually identical in eighty separate locations is hard to ignore. The detailed analysis of the photograph taken is another issue that is difficult to ignore.

March 30, 1990

Near Brussels, two F-16 pilots observed a UFO that was triangular in nature. It had the three white lights at each point of the triangle and a red light in the center as was reported from other sightings. The aircraft was tracked visually by the F-16s using their onboard radar, as well as by an observer on the ground. The aircraft was tracked going from 150 knots to almost 990 knots within a second.

This particular incident was confirmed by the F-16 pilot, the pilot's radar on board his aircraft, and by someone on the ground. Three independent sources at the same incident claim it took place as reported.[41]

January 27, 1991

A soldier in Iraq, codename JT, saw a triangular shape about one thousand feet long with lights at each point of the triangle. He was stationed near Hafar al-Batin and had been in the US Army for twenty-four years. His sighting was thought to be legitimate.[42]

1992

Michael Via, an intelligence analyst on board a ship in the Persian Gulf, saw a triangular aircraft in the daytime sky above the ship. The triangular craft was black with lights on each of its points and made absolutely no sound. Via observed the object from an observation point on the highest point of the mast. He said the ship was close enough that he could see every detail.

A highly trained individual who claims that it was daylight and he was on a high point of the ship where he clearly saw a triangular aircraft in detail reported this. It was not something far off in the distance, it was not at night or at dusk, and it was not just a blip on a radar screen. It was clearly visible, and unless we say this observation is a lie, how do we discount this sighting?[43]

2001

A computer systems administrator by the name of Gary McKinnon hacked into the US Space Command computer system and found a series of space photographs. They were in two files, one marked "filtered" and the other marked "unfiltered." When he opened the files, he found almost identical pictures. In the unfiltered file were pictures of alien spacecraft in space. In the filtered file, everything was identical except the spacecraft had been removed.

McKinnon continued to hack into government computers and claims that he eventually got into the NASA database. He claims to have seen pictures showing North America from space in which were a whole series of cigar-shaped spacecraft, each one about two football fields long. In addition, there were smaller scout craft in the pictures. He claims to have also seen pictures of ship-to-ship transfers of materials. It appeared as if this space force utilized antigravity propulsion systems and circled the earth.

There was an attempt to arrest McKinnon, but after an unsuccessful extradition attempt, charges were dropped.[44] McKinnon claims that this space force around the earth is made up of the eight massive, cigar-shaped spacecraft and forty-three smaller scout ships. Supposedly, this is part of a supersecret program known as Solar Warden, which in essence is a space-based weapon system.[45]

To support this claim I would want to have more than some pictures that were supposedly hacked from NASA. Certainly, if such a space force does exist, there must be other records of this major operation. What is hard to accept is that our technology would have progressed so far and so fast as to be able to have developed the cigar-shaped ships described. We have watched the shuttle program, and we are just now beginning to develop reusable rockets. To believe that we have advanced far beyond that and have a space force in place is, for me, a stretch. An even bigger stretch would be to accept that we are somehow cooperating with alien life-forms who either helped us make the equipment or provided the ships that make up this so-called space force. If it exists, why has it not been seen by astronauts on the International Space Station?

This hacker may have gotten into some files that had pictures of a planned space force. To accept that such a space force is already in existence and patrolling the skies above our country would require a lot more evidence.

November 14, 2004

On November 14, 2004, an aircraft carrier battle group, including the *Princeton* and the *Nimitz,* was tracking a series of unidentified areal phenomena (UAP). The air was filled with what looked like a fleet of spaceships hovering over the entire battle group. F-18s were no match for these Tic Tac–shaped craft, and it was clear that this fleet of UAPs, as they are now called, were observing the battle group. People are now coming forward to describe the unbelievable encounter that took place in November 2004. We now know that the Pentagon has a secret agency called the Advanced Aerospace Threat Identification Program (AATIP) that studies encounters between the military and UFOs. Congress has been holding secret hearings about the UFO sightings.[46]

Now let us jump ahead to the very recent past.

September 2019

Chris Mellon, formerly the deputy assistant secretary of defense for intelligence under both Bill Clinton and George W. Bush, interviewed a former army intelligence analyst (name withheld) about his sightings of alien aircraft in the Canyonlands National Park, in Utah. The analyst said the craft moved across the ground as if they were searching for something or mapping the area. He took pictures that were later analyzed and found to be authentic. The number of such sightings alarmed Mellon. Bill Scott of *Aviation Week* told Mellon that his magazine had plotted the sightings of these triangular aircraft and found that many of the sightings appeared to be over military bases, especially those with nuclear weapons, including bases in other countries all over the world. Chris Mellon also interviewed David Marler from Mutual UFO Network (MUFON), who had over seventeen thousand documented UFO sightings. Mr. Marler is the author of *Triangular UFO: An Estimate of the Situation.*

This reference is of particular interest due to the career of Chris Mellon. Throughout a very distinguished career, he has keenly focused on unconventional national threats. He now works as a civilian with a group called To the Stars Academy of Arts & Science. This group has been trying to encourage greater investigation by the US defense and intelligence communities concerning UFOs.

He said his motivation was due to the increasing number of such sightings, especially over sensitive military areas. He has received reports from many highly trained and credible witnesses. In addition, this information has been corroborated by some of the most leading-edge technology, including infrared video taken by fighter jet pilots. Mr. Mellon has stated that some of this indicates a high-level strategic threat posed by an unknown operator. The interface between Mr. Mellon and the History Channel is significant in the UFO investigation.

The 2004 aircraft carrier task force encounter and the top guns who tangled with a Tic Tac–shaped UFO are two of the more credible and outstanding incidents that Mellon investigated. There is the concern that the Russians or Chinese have leapfrogged over our technology and are responsible for some of these sightings. It is also possible that what we are observing is not of our world. It is clear, however, that the spacecraft seen in these encounters have capabilities far beyond what the United States currently possesses and are most likely beyond any earthly entity. Mr. Mellon has not come to any conclusion, but he does believe it is imperative that we investigate these UFOs and learn their origin and capabilities.[47]

July 25 and 27, 2020

The Department of Defense released videos from three encounters with aircraft that are being called *unidentified aerial phenomena* (UAP). Previously this information had been kept secret. The vehicles involved in these encounters are referred to as "off-world vehicles." Their capabilities far exceed anything that the United States has or that we believe any nation on Earth possesses.

In a July 25, 2020, article in *Popular Mechanics*, Andrew Daniels reported that Harry Reid, former Nevada Senator, believes that spacecraft from other worlds have crashed on our planet. He said material recovered from these crashes has been studied and used by government contractors for decades. This reinforces the claims of Colonel Corso, who contended that for two years he provided materials from the Roswell crash to contractors that were used in weapons and technology development. Reid's statement is also in agreement with the deathbed declaration of Norma Gardner, who claimed to have cataloged over a thousand items taken from alien crashes. Finally, it supports the deathbed declaration of former Lieutenant Haut, who confirmed the Roswell crash.

In June, the Senate held hearings concerning appropriations for this operation for fiscal year 2021. The government's UAP office currently resides in the Office of Naval Intelligence. The Unidentified Aerial Phenomena Task Force is meant to standardize and collect reporting on sightings and report on these twice a year. In recent years, there have been many reports of unidentified aircraft over many of our most sensitive military installations and cities. The frequency and detailed descriptions followed by radar contact and trained pilot observations make ignoring these sightings nearly impossible.[48]

In July 2020, the *New York Times* reported that Eric Davis, the astrophysicist who consulted on the UFO project, said some of the materials defense contractors had that he had examined came from **"off-world vehicles not made on this earth."**[49]

4

Trips to the Moon

The importance of discussing the moon landings rests in two areas. First are the sightings that some of our astronauts claim, when they saw both alien beings and spacecraft. The second issue is that if in fact aliens wanted to visit our planet, the side of the moon we cannot see from Earth would be an outstanding staging area for their exploration.

Following our first moon landing, which took place July 20, 1969, there were discussions as to what our astronauts saw during their visit to the moon. A two-minute break in communications did exist during the moonwalk of Neil Armstrong. Each astronaut, in addition to the normal communications channel, had a so-called medical communi-cations channel that was supposedly not monitored by news media. Radio hams in the United States claim that they in fact hacked into that medical channel and heard Neil Armstrong report that he saw not only alien beings but three alien spacecraft along the rim of a large crater next to the landing site of the *Eagle*. There is no doubt that when Neil Armstrong and Buzz Aldrin returned to Earth they seemed very sullen, especially Mr. Armstrong. Neither astronaut ever talked much about his experience on the moon.[50]

A man by the name of Bob Dean who was formerly the command sergeant major at SHAPE in NATO claimed that the United States government destroyed forty rolls of film that were taken on the Apollo 11 mission. Dr. Stephen Greer, founder of the Center of the Study for Extraterrestrial Intelligence, claims he knew of discussions between

Neil Armstrong and Buzz Aldrin and that they in fact did see aliens on the moon during Apollo 11.[51]

On July 23, 2008, astronaut Edgar Mitchell of Apollo 14 was interviewed on Britain's Kerrang! Radio. Mitchell said he believed witnesses who claimed to have seen creatures from another world at Roswell, New Mexico, in 1947 and that they told the truth. He also said that he had been privileged to top-secret information about the UFO phenomenon, and he believed we had been visited by extraterrestrial beings. Astronaut Mitchell also warned that there are stories that are not true, but that he knows that extraterrestrial beings have and are visiting planet Earth.[52]

When you combine his statement with the reluctance of people like Neil Armstrong and Buzz Aldrin to talk publicly about UFOs following their Apollo 11 mission, it is difficult to ignore the reality that most likely at least some of the alien sightings are accurate.

Have Astronauts Acknowledged Seeing Aliens?

Yes, some of them have seen aliens. During Neil Armstrong's first voyage to the moon, one of the astronauts in the spacecraft saw some strange creature with all its limbs spread outward coming toward them. He managed to capture it with his camera, but the glass window reflected light onto the lens and the image does not show the creature clearly. Astronauts (the word comes from the Greek meaning "star sailor") are some of the most highly trained people on Earth. Astronauts must have a BS degree in either engineering, biological science, physical science, computer science, or mathematics. They must have at least three years of work experience prior to joining NASA, and astronaut training at NASA takes two years. These individuals are taught to observe their surroundings and accurately report what they have seen. Therefore, by their training and by the level of trust that our government places in these individuals, to believe that they would purposefully lie about what they saw during their space exploration is not credible to me.

In addition to Edgar Mitchell, astronauts Gordon Cooper and Deke Slayton also claim they saw aliens during their time at NASA.[53]

Apollo 11 *Eagle* on the Moon (photo courtesy of NASA)

Apollo 11 Crew: Armstrong, Collins, and Aldrin
(photo courtesy of NASA)

US Astronaut Edgar Mitchell (photo courtesy of NASA)

US Astronaut Gordon Cooper (photo courtesy of NASA)

US Astronaut Deke Slayton (photo courtesy of NASA)

5

Most Important Evidence

The number of reported sightings of both alien vessels and aliens themselves is astounding. Certainly, some of these sightings have been crafted for publicity or possibly for financial reasons, but some, especially those that have been reported by reputable individuals, are hard to discount.

For me, one of the most troubling reports is the one about the US Navy patrol boats in Vietnam. From that report and from the evidence that was retrieved from the attack on the Australian ship the *Hobart*, it is clear that attacking alien craft may very well be futile and in fact dangerous. Some people claim that, with the advent of lasers and focused energy weapons, we now have the means to resist any such alien spacecraft. This ignores the very real possibility that such craft might have the ability to reflect back laser or focused energy weapons to their source.

If we accept that we are being visited by alien beings that have the capability of visiting Earth, then we also must acknowledge that their technology and most likely their defensive and offensive capabilities may make our efforts useless.

It is certainly understandable why governments, including the United States government, have been reluctant to release everything that is most likely known by world political authorities. We saw what happened in 1938 when H. G. Wells read his book *War of the Worlds* on radio: there were riots and panic all over the world.[54] The reaction that is most likely to occur if we have irrefutable contact with alien beings could be difficult to handle.

In recent years, there has been a lot of speculation as to what may be on the side of the moon that we are unable to see from Earth. It may be that some of our Apollo missions as well as the most recent exploration by the Chinese of the side of moon not visible from Earth show that there may be or have been alien bases on the moon. Unquestionably, if aliens intended to visit Earth, using the side of the moon that is not visible to us would be an outstanding location to establish an outpost.

More is being learned about the far side of the moon, such as about the topography, which is totally different than the side we can see from Earth. The portion of the moon that is hidden from our view is much more cratered, and scientists are looking at why this phenomenon exists. Below is a picture of the far side of the moon taken on the Apollo 14 mission; however, it does not seem to indicate any structures that could have been created by extraterrestrials. The interest in the far side of the moon, both from a geological perspective as well as regarding its possible use as a staging point by visitors to Earth, will continue as our technology becomes more sophisticated. If extraterrestrials have been using the far side of the moon as a base, it is very possible that is one reason for their increased sightings as they visit our planet to seek more information about our efforts.

Far side of moon, as viewed from *Apollo 14*
(photo courtesy of NASA)

One of the other more troubling incidents reported and documented was the appearance of what appeared to be a fleet of alien vessels above our carrier task force. It was almost as if they were saying to us, *Even your most powerful military force would be no match for a fleet of our spacecraft.* It is also clear from the observations of these alien craft that they have a number of shapes. We have the traditional flying saucer. We have some that look like a Tic Tac. Recently, there have been many sightings of equilateral-triangle-shaped spaceships. We have had a few sightings of larger vessels that look like motherships and one report of smaller vessels entering the larger one. The descriptions of these three shapes are so similar, it is difficult to discount these sightings. It is also hard to ignore the sightings by trained pilots and other individuals who are highly skilled and credible. The confirmation by radar of some sightings make them even more creditable.

The appearance of several vehicle shapes begs the question of whether these alien visitors are from the same planet, or is it possible that we are being visited by intelligent life from different planets? The number of sightings and the apparent willingness of these potential visitors to appear over our populated areas makes one wonder if they are about to make more direct contact in the near future. Certainly, our military and the military intelligence of other countries are concerned. It seems as if the efforts around the world to further document and identify these sightings are expanding. If these visitors turn hostile, it undoubtedly would be a way of unifying the world.

Another report that is most intriguing is of the pictures from hacker Gary McKinnon, who claims he got into NASA's files and found pictures of a space force named Solar Warden. He claims this force consists of cigar-shaped vessels about twice the size of a football field as well as smaller vessels, and they are supposedly protecting the earth. If this story is true, who built this system and what is its true purpose? Could it be something developed jointly by alien beings and earthlings? Is it something that the United States has developed in secret?[55]

As the government seems to be more forthcoming with sensitive information, as reported on July 27 and 29, 2020, we may soon find out.

Photos from iStock by Getty Images

One Final Piece of Critical Information: the Elongated Skulls

There is very little physical evidence that has been uncovered to document possible alien visitation. However, on October 25, 1927, what have become known as the Paracas elongated skulls were found in the Ica Region of Peru. That is why these seventeen skulls are so important when trying to establish the presence of aliens on our planet. Here we have potential physical evidence that could establish that extraterrestrials in fact did visit our planet in the past. There is some belief that this elongation may have been caused by a practice followed by some tribes of wrapping the heads of children to distort their heads.

In 2017, one of these skulls was analyzed by Todd Disotell, PhD, a molecular anthropologist at NYU. He could not find any sign of the sagittal sutures that are present on all human skulls. He used magnetic resonance imaging to see if there was any evidence of the suture that could not be seen on the surface, but none could be found. Dr. Disotell received permission to extract material from the teeth and sent it for DNA analysis.

The analysis was very difficult and took five years to complete. The results were just published May 31, 2020. The report said that the DNA taken from the teeth in these skulls was not human. The DNA did not fit *any known* evolutionary trees and was like nothing they had ever seen before. One interesting reality is that DNA existed in these skulls. It does show some sort of relationship between life on Earth and life in the greater universe.[56]

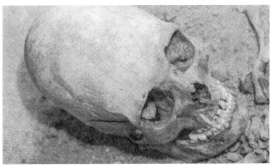

Photo from iStock by Getty Images

6

My Conclusions

When searching through the available data on UFOs, I tried to identify and remove information that did not appear credible or that had obvious contradictions; for example, the astronaut that was carved into the sixteenth-century cathedral which turned out to have been added by a worker in 1992. Regarding the incident reported by Gary McKinnon of a space force, I did acknowledge that he may have tapped into a database at NASA as he claims, but what he saw was something that was conceptual rather than in existence.

Some of the sightings stand alone without a lot of corroborating evidence but the individuals appear to be believable. In other cases, we have multiple sightings, we have radar intercepts, and, as in the case of the former lieutenant who created the cover story from Roswell and the airman who cataloged the alien artifacts at Wright-Patterson Air Force Base, we have their deathbed statements acknowledging their claims as true. We also have YouTube evidence of Barry Goldwater's discussion with his friend Gen. Curtis LeMay telling him never to mention UFOs to him again.

I consider the following information to be of most importance in helping me come to an opinion concerning extraterrestrial intelligent life visiting the earth:

- First was the book written by Colonel Corso about the Roswell incident. I independently verified the extensive claims made by the colonel with respect to all of the figures involved in his book and the 1947 Roswell incident. In each case, the colonel's description of who they were and what they did was verified by several other sources, and it appears that everything he stated about the individuals he identified was factual.

- The 2007 deathbed statement of Lieutenant Haut, who was responsible for producing the cover story at Roswell of the weather balloon. In his statement, the former lieutenant said there was a crash at Roswell in 1947. He saw the spacecraft at White Sands as well as dead alien bodies as they were taken to the autopsy room. Also, the deathbed statement of Norma Gardner, who claimed that she not only cataloged more than a thousand items taken from alien crashes, but also personally saw alien bodies stored in glass containers at Wright-Patterson Air Force Base.

- The statements from three astronauts that they had seen aliens in conjunction with their explorations for NASA. To discount the direct statements of astronauts Edgar Mitchell, Gordon Cooper, and Deke Slayton is, for me, a stretch too far. These individuals and the nature of their careers make it impossible for me to believe that they all would be lying about something as crucial as seeing aliens during their space explorations.

- The January 1978 incident at McGuire Air Force Base, where an alien was shot by a military policeman; everything being confirmed by an air force major. Additionally, I studied reports of UFO sightings by trained law enforcement officials in general, who were taught to make observations and accurately report and document what they have seen, and I find them very unlikely to be incorrect or falsified.

- The June 1968 encounter in Vietnam was extremely

compelling. Many details were recorded of this incident that caused the navy to investigate what took place and prepare an after-action report that resulted in directions to both US Air Force and Navy pilots not to engage alien aircraft in the future.

- The account of the Japanese pilot of flight 1628 about his encounter with both two small alien aircraft and a huge spaceship was extremely detailed, and tapes were made between him and the tower at Anchorage during this encounter. Both the pilot and the co-pilot were seasoned professionals, and the pilot provided drawings of what he had seen in an encounter that lasted about fifty minutes. All of the information, including radar data and eye-witness reports, were reviewed by the deputy director of the FAA, which resulted in his telling everyone involved not to talk of this incident, and stating that "it never happened," which lends credibility to this encounter.

- The analysis of the November 1989 photograph taken of an alien aircraft during the Belgian wave, during which 150 sightings in eighty locations were reported. The photograph was studied for a year and found to be genuine. As part of the work done on the photograph, it was subjected to infrared examination, which showed evidence that what powered the aircraft was believed to be an electromagnetic propulsion system.

- The 1992 sighting by a trained intelligence analyst on board a vessel at sea in broad daylight was extremely detailed and compelling.

- The 2004 encounter of a sky full of flying saucers by the aircraft battle group is an incident that is impossible to ignore. The fastest aircraft we had at the time, F-18s, were incapable of keeping up with the alien craft. Thousands of naval personnel observed this encounter.

- The interviews and analysis of Mr. Chris Mellon, whose reputation and significant position as the deputy assistant secretary for intelligence, clearly indicated that alien aircraft had visited us.

The final convincing incident was the admission by the Department of Defense that the United States Navy had three encounters with UFOs, as well as the conclusion by the astrophysicist who was part of the original UFO project, Eric Davis, that he saw unusual items in the hands of defense contractors and that, as he said, these items came from "off-world vehicles not made on this earth."

It would be inappropriate for me to ask you to decide without sharing my conclusions with you. After a careful assessment of all the data to date, it is clear to me that we have been visited for a long period of time by extraterrestrial beings. Further, the increased frequency of these visits and their apparent willingness to appear around populated areas, for me, is conclusive evidence of their existence. I believe the most important aspect is not the total volume of people who have reported incidents, but the number of people who corroborated some of the key incidents with almost identical details.

I trust this book addressed many of your concerns and contained the data you needed to make an informed decision about the question, What, if anything, is out there?

7

Analysis from a Military Perspective

Now that I have provided some historical background and information about reported sightings, let us look at the question of how we would deal with an alien force from a military perspective if in fact we were visited by extraterrestrial intelligent life. It is the purpose of our military to defend this country against any potential threat. Thus, an analysis of the possible danger posed to our country by intelligent life-forms is essential.

I have chosen to view this from a military perspective because of my thirty years' experience in the US Army. I want to provide the reader with my background not to brag or ingratiate myself but to provide some context of the experience that I was fortunate enough to acquire during my military career. In particular, my training at the War College and my understanding of how the military functions at the higher levels gave me the insight to prepare this analysis.

First, I completed my bachelor's degree in finance and was a Distinguished Military Graduate from Penn State. I was commissioned as a second lieutenant in the Regular Army in July 1963. The following year I completed my MBA at Lehigh University. My first assignment in the military was in field artillery in an eight-inch self-propelled howitzer battalion. Upon reporting to my unit, I was informed by the battalion commander that my assignment would be the nuclear weapons officer. At the time, the facts that my artillery battalion was a nuclear delivery unit and possessed those weapons were top secret. As such, my position required a top-secret crypto clearance predicated on an extensive background investigation.

In addition to being responsible for the training of our nuclear weapons specialists, I was responsible for overseeing the actual security of the nuclear warheads. I was part of the nuclear release authority called Permissive Action Link (PAL). This system begins with the president and then follows a dual track requiring two officers at each military echelon to authenticate the release of nuclear weapons. I also received nuclear weapons and combat intelligence training in Germany. I spent almost two years in that assignment in Hanau, Germany, and later became a finance officer at Fort Lewis, Washington. I completed the Command and General Staff College, which concentrates on military tactics. In 1981, I was recalled to active duty to head the development of the pay system for the Army Reserve and National Guard.

Starting with captain, my promotions came at an accelerated rate, and after nineteen years I attained the rank of colonel. Two years later, I was selected to attend the Army War College in Carlisle, Pennsylvania. This is the highest-level school for commissioned officers and is designed to prepare senior officers to serve on the joint staff of the secretary of defense. The purpose of the training is to develop the skills to make recommendations on military and geopolitical issues to the most senior military and civilian authorities.

In 1985, I was nominated for brigadier general after receiving numerous recommendations from two general officers. However, because of my nuclear weapons experience, I was never assigned to Vietnam. This lack of combat experience was most likely the reason for my not being promoted to general officer. The final assignment I had in the military was as the commander of the United States Finance Support Agency. This specialized army unit handled the financial operations for an engaged military force of up to five hundred thousand troops. After my departure from active duty, I was approved for Senior Executive Service level positions in the federal government. In 1968,

I was awarded the Army Commendation Medal; I was awarded the Meritorious Service Medal in 1983 and again in 1993. I retired as a colonel in July 1993.

1LT Gene P. Abel, Germany 1965

Col. Gene P. Abel, July 26, 1982

- Military planning has developed over the years into a very sophisticated and comprehensive process. It is based on learning as much as possible about a possible adversary. Insight into the capabilities and probable actions of an adversary is the primary focus of military planning.

Some of the most important areas that are looked at are the following:

- The weapons, both their capability and quantity, of any potential adversary.
- Probable tactics and knowledge of the senior military command.
- Their capability for logistics and communications.

One of the most intriguing elements of military planning today is a thing called Order of Battle. This amounts to amassing information about the most senior command of your enemy in an attempt to predict how they will react in a particular situation. One great example of this goes back to General Lee and his knowledge about General Grant during the Civil War. These generals attended West Point together and knew each other. During the war, after some of the victories Grant had in the West, some of the Confederate generals said they believed Grant would simply fade into the background after his successes. Lee, on the other hand, knowing more about Grant's personality, told them that was not what Grant would do. Lee said General Grant would never quit. As it turned out, Lee was correct, and even though it did not enable the South to win the Civil War, it is an example of knowing your opponents to better predict what they might do.

Another example from the Civil War is the issue of logistics. For the military to function they need huge amounts of everything. During the Civil War, the South had a very limited capacity to produce the kinds of equipment and supplies needed for the war. On the other hand, the North had the industrial capability to produce the weapons and materials necessary to conduct a prolonged fight, and that was one of the factors contributing to the North winning the war.

Another important element is for a country who wants to win a military engagement to have superior forces both on the ground (and sea) and in the air. The air force dubs this "to achieve and maintain air superiority." With this information, the military develops a strategy and then the tactics necessary to make the strategy successful.

At this point, we cannot say that the intelligent life that would most likely land and observe our world is hostile; however, there is certainly the potential for such a situation to develop. From my research, I have found nothing, with the exception of the incident in Vietnam in 1968, that showed any direct hostile interaction between earthlings and our visitors from space. Even in this situation, it appears that the aliens simply returned the weapons that we were using against them. They did not initiate military action. The closest they came to initiating hostilities was the day following the initial attacks on the patrol boats, when all of a sudden three missiles fired the preceding day at the spacecraft by our F-4s struck the Australian ship the *Hobart*.

Using the techniques that the military employs to develop strategies and tactics to defend our country, we would look at how they might apply to a situation to deal with intelligent life from outside our planet.

If we began with assessing the type and quantity of weapons that they possess, we truly would have a very great void. Since they have not used any offensive tactics against us, the only experience that we have with respect to their weaponry is their apparent ability to redirect weapons that we fired at them back toward us. If this is not an isolated incident, which we have no reason to believe that it is, conventional weaponry would appear to be very ineffective and in fact hazardous to use against any alien aircraft. This was the conclusion that the Department of Defense came to after analyzing the event in Vietnam in 1968. After that analysis, a directive was issued to air force and navy pilots, ordering them not to engage UFOs.

The apparent ability to deflect and redirect weapons back to the source is also something that might affect some of the less conventional weapons that we have developed, specifically focused energy beams and lasers. One of the advantages of these two types of weapons is the speed with which they travel; they would most likely be able to engage enemy spacecraft even with the ability to move at speeds that we cannot begin to match. Since these weapons travel at the speed of light, they might be employed effectively against an alien vessel. What we do not have data about, and have no way of knowing at this point, is whether or not their defensive systems would be capable of redirecting and deflecting even lasers or particle beam weapons.

It is possible that from some of the UFO crashes our scientists have a better idea as to the effectiveness of our more exotic weapons on an enemy spacecraft. Certainly, this would be a crucial determination with respect to the tactics we might use to defend ourselves against an alien attack. According to Colonel Corso's book, one of the major objectives of reverse engineering and providing alien technology to our defense contractors was to determine how to deal with our unearthly opponents and their alien spacecraft.

Another issue is the idea of supply and logistics. From the number of sightings we have observed and from a few cases where large numbers of alien aircraft appeared, such as the incident with the aircraft carrier task force, it would appear that they have the capability to supply whatever they would need. From the observations of smaller craft being supplied from or entering into a larger mothership, they may in fact have a very sophisticated supply and logistics capability. As to their ability to communicate, the fact that they can move in tandem with one another at extreme rates of speed, which we have observed and documented on radar, indicates their communications capability is both integrated and extremely effective.

With all this superiority, one question that comes to mind is, Why do we believe numerous alien spaceships have crashed on Earth? We can only conjecture that even though the alien technology is far ahead of what we possess, it is a device and there are thinking beings aboard. Therefore, there is the potential for alien error together with the failure of the technology and systems that they have developed. A series of severe lightning storms took place at Roswell in 1947 on the day of the crash. It is conceivable that lightning or other natural forces could have affected even their sophisticated aircraft.

The element of understanding the nature of an opponent and what they might do in any situation is nonexistent. We have never met these beings one on one. Given the lack of any direct knowledge or contact with the aliens, it is impossible to know what their leaders might do in any particular situation. However, as we have observed, they appear simply to be watching and surveying the earth. On a number of sightings, it was noted that they appeared to be moving in a logical pattern, as if they were looking for something or trying to scan or map a section of the ground. Why they would be visiting the earth is a perplexing issue, but we certainly can develop some insight if we accept the fact that they have been visiting us for many years, as some of the drawings in caves and on temples seem to indicate. It may be their curiosity is similar to us going to the moon and our desire to visit Mars. We did not go to the moon to fight a war but to learn more about the planets and bodies that surround our planet.

Everything we have seen so far with respect to the duration of their visits to our planet and what they were doing on these visits indicates that they are trying to learn more about both Earth and now its inhabitants. It is also possible that as they observed what was going on, they saw the inhabitants of Earth developing things like nuclear weapons and wanted to have a better understanding of our actions. The fact that so many sightings have been at nuclear facilities in different countries of the world makes me wonder if they are concerned about what we are doing. Another possibility is that the aliens are identifying their location if a future action might require neutralizing those weapons.

Although we have not been able to ascertain as much as we would like about their vulnerability, we have examples of them being killed by something as simple as a .45 or an M1 rifle. We have the report from Roswell that a soldier shot and killed one of the aliens with his M1, and we have the incident at McGuire Air Force Base where an alien was shot and killed with a .45-caliber handgun. This would surely indicate that the aliens themselves are prone to the same danger as humans once they are not in their ships. We also have not observed these beings in any elaborate spacesuit but merely wearing a fabric garment, like the aliens at Roswell. We do not even know if our planet's viruses or bacteria would adversely affect them.

Analyzing what they might do in the future is best approached from the perspective that there seems to be an increasing number of sightings with the concentration of sightings over sensitive military locations. It is certainly possible that sometime in the near future they will choose to either make direct contact with people on Earth or, in the worst possible scenario, initiate offensive military action.

We now know that the United States has been conducting a detailed study of UFOs, and there is obviously a great deal of concern with respect to their sightings in the increased frequency of these reports. The concern of President Harry Truman was made clear by his creating Majestic 12 and sending our highest-level military and scientific minds to Roswell, New Mexico, to study the possible crash of an alien vessel. Secrecy and the outright refusal to acknowledge sightings that were seen by scores or even hundreds of people indicated that the government was concerned about the aliens and the reaction of the people if it became clear we were being visited by intelligent life.

Given the fact that we have observed at least three distinct configurations of vessels, surely the military is considering the implication: Do these different types of spaceships come from the same source, or could it be that we have had visitors from multiple intelligent societies? If different alien groups are visiting us, the difficulty of our situation is compounded. Trying to determine the possible actions and strategy of one alien is hard enough. It is certainly possible that the visits are coming from the same source and they have just developed different types of spaceships, the same way that we have developed different types of aircraft.

Another issue that the military must be analyzing is the large number of sightings and in some cases the large quantities of UFOs in one location. Where are they operating from in the universe? Speculation of course is that they may be utilizing the side of the moon that is not visible from Earth. Although we have not acknowledged any structures that appear to have been constructed by intelligent life, it would make all the tactical sense in the world to locate a base where we cannot observe what they are doing. If they have chosen this option, to operate from the moon, it very possible that they have chosen to construct the facilities underground. This would make them nearly impossible to observe even with the new spacecraft and land rovers that we have developed to explore the moon.

I suspect that one piece of information that will be crucial to future moon landings will be a greater examination of the far side of the moon to see whether or not aliens have established a base of operations there. One other possibility that I am sure is being considered is the report from the hacker that claims there is a space force surrounding the earth consisting of cigar-shaped vessels and smaller shuttlecraft. If this exists, is it something the United States could have developed and kept secret, or is it possible that aliens have made contact with people on Earth and provided help to construct such a defensive system as the hacker into the NASA files claims to have discovered?

Conventional military analysis of possible alien intentions is hampered by the lack of information that we would otherwise possess about an adversary on Earth. One thing, however, is certainly very clear: the knowledge and technology that would be necessary to come from great distances to visit Earth and to perform some of the feats we have seen show the superiority of their technology. Just how superior is the issue. We can only hope that analysis of some of the spacecraft that we believe have crashed has provided some answers as to their capabilities. Our ability to effectively deal with them is critical should they become hostile.

It is important that the Department of Defense has acknowledged that we have not only had encounters with UFOs but that we have been investigating this ongoing phenomenon. The challenge this could present to the world in the future may be like none other we have experienced.

Science-fiction writers, like H. G. Wells, have provided us with possible scenarios. I remember a science-fiction movie in which aliens come to Earth supposedly in friendship. When they first arrive, they give the people a book with what they say is their reason for visiting Earth, which is written in a language that the humans can't decipher. At the end of this movie, scientists are able to decode the language used in the book and it turns out to be a cookbook entitled "How to Serve Man." In other sci-fi movies the aliens desire to live on Earth and to do so they would need to eliminate the human race. Still others claim the aliens are looking for minerals and other things that they need for their own civilization.

At this point, all of this is conjecture, but for me the most compelling element seems to be the increasing number of UFO sightings and the fact that many of these occurrences are being carried out over population centers where many people have observed their visits. This might indicate an intent to make contact in the near future—whether that be done peacefully or not.

We had better hope that if their intent becomes hostile, the information we have derived from their crashes has enabled us to provide defensive weaponry that is effective and able to deter any offensive military actions. If not, our other problems will pale in comparison.

Photos from iStock by Getty Images

NOTES

INTRODUCTION

1. Siegel, "The Most Distant Galaxy Ever Discovered by NASA's Hubble Space Telescope."
2. Garner, "Nancy Grace Roman Space Telescope."

CHAPTER 1

3. Schoch, "Robert Schoch: Research Highlights: The Great Sphinx."
4. "Wikipedia: London Hammer."
5. "Britannica: Hans Lippershey."
6. History, "Galileo Galilei."
7. Evon and Mikkelson, "Astronaut Carving Found on Ancient Spanish Cathedral."

CHAPTER 2

8. Corso, *The Day After Roswell*, 1–6.
9. Sleppy, affidavit.
10. Twining, "The Twining Memo."
11. "The Many Stories of Lt. Haut."
12. "Lieutenant Walter Haut's Deathbed Confession."
13. Randle, "A Little Help with Norma Gardner."
14. "The Majestic 12."
15. Dolan, "The Death of James Forrestal."
16. Corso, *The Day After* Roswell, 41.
17. Orbman, "Philip Corso's Claim of Seeing Alien Bodies."
18. Publications International, "History of the Roswell UFO Incident."
19. Corso, *The Day After Roswell*, 47–50.
20. Corso, *The Day After Roswell*, 4.
21. "The Roswell 'Witness' List."

Chapter 3

22. "Project BLUE BOOK – Unidentified Flying Objects."
23. Meares, "The Unsolved Mystery of the Lubbock Lights UFO Sightings."
24. Booth, "The Lubbock Lights, 1951."
25. Randle, "A Little Help with Norma Gardner."
26. "The Levelland Sightings (Texas)."
27. Booth, "The 1965 Kecksburg, Pennsylvania Crash."
28. *UFO Conspiracy: Hunt for the Truth.*
29. Robinson, "Barry Goldwater on Curtis LeMay and UFOs."
30. Waring, "Sheriffs Have UFO Sighting of Craft Making Impossible Maneuvers."
31. Klotz and Salas, "The Malmstrom AFB UFO/Missile Incident."
32. *UFO Conspiracy: Hunt for the Truth.*
33. History, "Jimmy Carter Files Report on UFO Sighting."
34. Hall, "Alien Being Shot Dead by MPs."
35. *UFO Conspiracy: Hunt for the Truth.*
36. Spiegel, "Retired Air Force Colonel Claims New Evidence Will Blow the Lid Off Rendlesham UFO Sighting."
37. *UFO Conspiracy: Hunt for the Truth.*
38. "Wikipedia: Japan Airlines Flight 1628 incident."
39. *Secret Access: UFOs on the Record.*
40. Lowth, "The Belgian UFO Wave."
41. Lange, "30 Years Later."
42. *Unidentified*
43. *Unidentified*
44. "Hacker Gary McKinnon Turns into a Search Expert."
45. Knox, "Evidence of an American Space Warship Force."
46. "Wikipedia: Pentagon UFO videos."
47. Hopkins, "Former US Defense Official."
48. Daniels, "Pentagon's UFO Group Is Officially Active."
49. "Ex-Pentagon Official."

CHAPTER 4

50. Richard, "Did Armstrong & Aldrin See Two Huge UFOs on the Moon?"
51. Monzon, "Retired Army Officer."
52. Booth, "Astronaut Edgar Mitchell."
53. "NASA Astronauts Say Aliens Are Watching Earth."

CHAPTER 5

54. Dixon, "'War of the Worlds' Broadcast Causes Chaos in 1938."
55. *UFO Conspiracy: Hunt for the Truth*.
56. "We Have DNA Results of the Paracas Elongated Skulls."

BIBLIOGRAPHY

Booth, B. J. "The 1965 Kecksburg, Pennsylvania Crash." UFO Casebook https://www.ufocasebook.com/Kecksburg.html.

Booth, B. J. "The Lubbock Lights, 1951." UFO Casebook. https://www.ufocasebook.com/lubbocklights.html.

Booth, Billy. "Astronaut Edgar Mitchell: 'UFOs Are Real.'" Live About. February 7, 2019. https://www.liveabout.com/astronaut-edgar-mitchell-ufos-are-real-3293680.

"Britannica: Hans Lippershey (Dutch inventor)." Encyclopædia Britannica. Updated November 25, 2019. https://www.britannica.com/biography/Hans-Lippershey.

Cooper, Helene, Leslie Kean, and Ralph Blumenthal. "2 Navy Airmen and an Object That 'Accelerated Like Nothing I've Ever Seen.'" *The New York Times*, December 16, 2017. https://www.nytimes.com/2017/12/16/us/politics/unidentified-flying-object-navy.html.

Corso, Col. (Ret.) Philip J. *The Day After Roswell.* (New York: Pocket Books, 1997).

Daniels, Andrew. "Pentagon's UFO Group Is Officially Active, After Years of Secrecy." *Popular Mechanics.* August 16, 2020. https://www.popularmechanics.com/military/research/a33614916/pentagon-ufo-task-force-active/#:~:text=Inside%20the%20Pentagon%27s%20Secret%20UFO%20Program%20In%20a,Deputy%20Secretary%20of%20Defense%2C%20approved%20the%20task%20force.

Dixon, George. "'War of the Worlds' Broadcast Causes Chaos in 1938." *New York Daily News.* October 29, 2015. Originally published by *Daily News*, October 31, 1938. https://www.

nydailynews.com/news/national/war-worlds-broadcast-caos-1938-article-1.2406951

Dolan, Richard M. "The Death of James Forrestal." Unknown Country. November 11, 2001. https://www.unknowncountry.com/insight/the-death-of-james-forrestal/.

Evon, Dan, and David Mikkelson. "Astronaut Carving Found on Ancient Spanish Cathedral." Snopes. January 18, 2009. https://www.snopes.com/fact-check/a-spanish-mystery/.

"Ex-Pentagon Official: 'Off-World Vehicles Have Been Found.'" Microsoft News. July 24, 2020. https://www.msn.com/en-us/news/technology/ex-pentagon-official-off-world-vehicles-have-been-found/ar-BB179ZYP.

Garner, Rob, ed. "Nancy Grace Roman Space Telescope." NASA. May 20, 2020. https://www.nasa.gov/content/goddard/nancy-grace-roman-space-telescope.

"Hacker Gary McKinnon Turns into a Search Expert." BBC. July 28, 2014. https://www.bbc.com/news/technology-28524909.

Hall, Richard. "Alien Being Shot Dead by MPs, January 18, 1978 (Ft. Dix & McGuire)." Edited by B. J. Booth. UFO Casebook. https://www.ufocasebook.com/ftdix.html#:~:text=Alien%20Being%20Allegedly%20Killed%20at%20Fort%20Dix.%20Alien,Jersey%20State%20Police%20who%20were%20searching%20for%20something.

History.com editors. "Galileo Galilei." History. July 23, 2010. https://www.history.com/topics/inventions/galileo-galilei.

History.com editors. "Jimmy Carter Files Report on UFO Sighting." History. November 16, 2009. https://www.history.com/this-day-in-history/carter-files-report-on-ufo-sighting.

Hopkins, Anna. "Former US Defense Official: We Know UFOs Are Real – Here's Why That's Concerning." Fox News. May 29,

2019. https://www.foxnews.com/science/christopher-mellon-official-ufo-sightings-real.

Klotz, Jim, and Robert Salas. "The Malmstrom AFB UFO/Missile Incident." CUFON. November 27, 1996. http://cufon.org/cufon/malmstrom/malm1.htm.

Knox, Patrick. "A Brit Hacker Famed for the Biggest Ever Breach of Top Secret US Computers Has Claimed to Have Seen Evidence of an American Space Warship Force." *Daily Star*. December 8, 2015. https://www.dailystar.co.uk/news/latest-news/star-wars-gary-mckinnon-hacker-17223516.

Lange, Jeva. "30 Years Later, We Still Don't Know What Really Happened During the Belgian UFO Wave." *The Week*. March 30, 2020. https://theweek.com/articles/905215/30-years-later-still-dont-know-what-really-happened-during-belgian-ufo-wave.

"The Levelland Sightings (Texas)." UFO Evidence. http://www.ufoevidence.org/cases/case228.htm.

"Lieutenant Walter Haut's Deathbed Confession." UFO Casebook. https://www.ufocasebook.com/hautconfession.html.

Lowth, Marcus. "The Belgian UFO Wave – A Truly Unique Display of the Unknown." UFO Insight. March 12, 2018. https://www.ufoinsight.com/ufos/waves/belgian-ufo-wave.

"The Majestic 12." Biblioteca Pleyades. November 22, 2005. https://www.bibliotecapleyades.net/sociopolitica/esp_sociopol_mj12_19.htm.

"The Many Stories of Lt. Haut." The Roswell Files. http://roswell-files.com/Witnesses/hautstory.htm.

Meares, Hadley. "The Unsolved Mystery of the Lubbock Lights UFO Sightings." History. August 8, 2018. https://www.history.com/news/lubbock-lights-ufo-sightings.

Monzon, Inigo. "Retired Army Officer: NASA Covered Up Apollo 11 UFO Encounter by Deleting Photos." *International Business Times*. July 11, 2019. https://www.ibtimes.com/retired-army-officer-nasa-covered-apollo-11-ufo-encounter-deleting-photos-2805955.

"NASA Astronauts Say Aliens Are Watching Earth." UNILAD. April 6, 2017. https://www.unilad.co.uk/science/nasa-astronauts-say-aliens-are-watching-earth/.

Orbman, "Philip Corso's Claim of Seeing Alien Bodies." Think Aboutit. August 6, 2014. http://www.thinkaboutitdocs.com/philip-corsos-claim-of-seeing-alien-bodies/.

"Project BLUE BOOK – Unidentified Flying Objects." National Archives. Last updated September 29, 2020. https://www.archives.gov/research/military/air-force/ufos.

Publications International, Ltd., editors. "History of the Roswell UFO Incident." How Stuff Works. https://science.howstuffworks.com/space/aliens-ufos/history-roswell-incident.htm.

Randle, Kevin. "A Little Help with Norma Gardner." *A Different Perspective* (blog). February 22, 2016. https://kevinrandle.blogspot.com/2016/02/a-little-help-with-norma-gardner.html.

Richard. "Did Armstrong & Aldrin See Two Huge UFOs on the Moon? The Facts Are Hard to Dispute." Educating Humanity. August 26, 2012. http://www.educatinghumanity.com/2012/08/Neil-Armstrong-Dead-Did-He-See-UFOs-Moon.html.

Robinson, Paul. "Barry Goldwater on Curtis LeMay and UFOs." YouTube. April 2, 2009. https://www.youtube.com/watch?v=gP-FBg1NNUBU.

"The Roswell 'Witness' List." NICAP. https://www.nicap.org/roswell-list.htm.

Schoch, Robert M. "Robert Schoch: Research Highlights: The Great Sphinx." Robert Schoch's official website. https://www.robert-schoch.com/sphinx.html.

Secret Access: UFOs on the Record. Aired August 25, 2011, on History Channel.

Siegel, Ethan. "The Most Distant Galaxy Ever Discovered by NASA's Hubble Space Telescope." *Forbes.* April 20, 2020. https://www.forbes.com/sites/startswithabang/2020/04/20/the-most-distant-galaxy-ever-discovered-by-nasas-hubble-space-telescope/#5387b5752c34.

Sleppy, Lydia A. Affidavit dated September 14, 1993. Ufologie. https://ufologie.patrickgross.org/rw/w/lydiasleppy.htm.

Spiegel, Lee. "Retired Air Force Colonel Claims New Evidence Will Blow the Lid Off Rendlesham UFO Sighting." *HuffPost.* July 21, 2015. https://www.huffpost.com/entry/retired-air-force-col-charles-halt-claims-new-evidence-will-blow-the-lid-off-rendlesham-forest-ufo-sighting_n_55a6c05ae4b04740a3dede3e.

Twining, Gen. Nathan. "The Twining Memo." The Roswell Files. http://www.roswellfiles.com/FOIA/twining.htm.

UFO Conspiracy: Hunt for the Truth. Aired July 7, 2017, on History Channel.

Unidentified: Inside America's UFO Investigation. Season 2, episode 2, "The Triangle Mystery." Aired July 18, 2020, on History Channel.

Waring, Scott C. "Sheriffs Have UFO Sighting of Craft Making Impossible Maneuvers, Michigan, USA March 14, 1966." UFOs Uncovered. https://ufosuncovered.com/ufo-information/sheriffs-have-ufo-sighting-of-craft-making-impossible-maneuvers-michigan-usa-march-14-1966.

"We Have DNA Results of the Paracas Elongated Skulls Discovered in Peru." *True Blog*. May 31, 2020. https://trueblog.net/we-have-dna-results-of-the-paracas-elongated-skulls-discovered-in-peru-4607/.

"Wikipedia: Japan Airlines Flight 1628 incident." Wikimedia Foundation. Last modified September 22, 2020. https://en.wikipedia.org/wiki/Japan_Airlines_Flight_1628_incident.

"Wikipedia: London Hammer." Wikimedia Foundation. Last modified September 6, 2020. https://en.wikipedia.org/wiki/London_Hammer.

"Wikipedia: Pentagon UFO videos." Wikimedia Foundation. Last modified September 25, 2020. https://en.wikipedia.org/wiki/Pentagon_UFO_videos.